"HOLD MY HAND LORD"

BY JOAN DADSWELL

Published by New Generation Publishing in 2013

Copyright © Joan Dadswell 2013

The author asserts the moral right under the Copyright, Designs and Patents Act 1988 to be identified as the author of this work.

All Rights reserved. No part of this publication may be reproduced, stored in a retrieval system or transmitted, in any form or by any means without the prior consent of the author, nor be otherwise circulated in any form of binding or cover other than that which it is published and without a similar condition being imposed on the subsequent purchaser.

www.newgeneration-publishing.com

 New Generation **Publishing**

About the Author

Joan was born in Fordingbridge, Hampshire in 1929, the youngest of a family of nine children; although attending the local Church of England Sunday school, it was not until after being married fifteen years and with six children of her own, that at the age of thirty-six, Joan became a committed Christian. She went on to become an accredited Methodist local preacher a few years later and is still preaching on occasions.

In 2005 Joan made her first short missionary trip to Kosovo, working with widows and children, this was followed with three more longer trips to Kosovo and one to Uganda.

Three of her favourite quotes are: "Age is no barrier in the service of Our Lord", "If you are willing, God will make you able" and "If you want to walk on the water you have got to get out of the boat."

Dedication

All of us, when we set out on a mission, ponder where we are going and what we are setting out to achieve, also need to have in mind all that we require for the task.

In writing this book I knew that I would need help. The writing of the sermonettes, prayers and poems, with God's help and the guidance of the Holy Spirit, I was sure would all fall into place but editing it etc was a different cup of tea.

I would need some help with proof-reading, punctuation, grammar etc but when it comes to lay out, type, format, etc, I am a lost cause. But like the advert, I know a man/lady who can. So it was then I went to find Sue who is a whizz-kid on this front and it is to her I dedicate this book.

Her dedication, her loyalty, her oneness with her Lord and with me brought, "Hold My Hand Lord" into its final state and I thank Sue very sincerely for all that she gave of her talent and herself to make this book possible.

May God bless all who read and ponder the words that have been written in Christian love.

Contents

About the Author 3
Dedication 5
Hold My Hand Lord 9
Majestic Over All The Earth (Psalm 8) 10
Come Unto Me 11
The Emmaus Road 12
John 17: v 21 13
Give Us This Day Our Daily Bread 16
John 12: v 32 17
Follow Me 19
Even into old age, we are his disciples 22
Why Lord? 23
Sun Shine 24
Let Us Pray 25
John 15: v 13 26
Does Nobody Else Care 28
Let God In! 29
Why Peter? 31
Prayer for New Beginnings 32
When You Hurt Someone You Love 34
The Peace Of The Lord 35
Prayer For A Hurting World 36
Stormy Waters 37
In Whatsoever State 38
In The Vineyard Of Our Lord 39
Life with No End 40

Walking Through The Valley 42
Never A Moment Out of His Care...44

Hold My Hand Lord

As we live our lives for our Lord, it is simple to look back over our Christian life and pick out or remember some times when we walked through the valley, we can see that Our Lord was right there guiding us through those darker times. There were those mountain top experiences, when all was well with our souls and again we can see that, indeed, Our Lord was there to rejoice with us.

Most of us can remember and say with confidence, *'Yes, indeed, our prayers had been answered and we can relate events to prove it!'*

But what of everyday life, when days seem, what we would call, ordinary, with no great event, good or bad to relate. Surely these are the days when we, perhaps, find it a bit more difficult to notice His presence, more difficult to witness to His love, mercy and blessings. These are the times we need to be reminded that there is never a moment when we are out of His care; never a moment when He does not *'..hold our hand.'*

It is in the journeying of everyday life that we sometimes need to be reminded of God's love for us, and the many promises that are there in His word for us. Through *'Hold My Hand Lord,'* I want to remind you and myself of some of those treasures contained in His word, that we may walk every day, our hand in His and filled anew with His Spirit.

I pray that as you read *'Hold My Hand Lord,'* you will be reminded again of all the wonderful promises of God to each and every one of us, also that you will be encouraged to claim and reclaim, time and time again, all the treasures that can be ours from the hands of God himself.

God Bless you all, Joan.

Majestic Over All The Earth

Psalm 8

Father God, the whole of the world is yours,
    you reign supreme in all the earth.
Your name is praised over all other names silencing your
    enemies as they behold how we,
    your children praise and worship you.
When I think of your creation,
    see the beauty of the sky,
        watch the sun and moon as they travel across the sky,
        see the stars sparkling in the night sky,
        each in their appointed place,
Can you really have time to bother with us,
    just mere mortals?
But you do bother about us,
    we are placed just a little lower than your angels.
    we are your children, your glory.
You love us with an endless love,
    our every breath is your concern.

You have placed the world into our safe keeping.
Trusting us with the care of your creation,
    all the animals, tame and wild,
    big and small, even tiny insects.
The birds of the air and all the fish that swim in the
    waters of the world.
You grant us the privilege of looking after everything
    that you have made,
        from the tallest mountain to the deepest valley,
        from towering trees to the smallest blades of grass.
All are ours to tend and care for.
Father God, we praise you, we worship you,
    we adore you.
You are our God.
We are your children.

                                                                 Amen.

Come Unto Me

I'm tired Lord, really tired. Life has been so busy lately and so many people, friends and family, all with problems that need to be addressed.

Why do they always all come together, never separately, never on their own? Where does one begin, who needs attention first? The question asked so often, *'Are you free next ....?' 'Would you be able to please .....?'* Of course I am free, of course I will. Then you remember you were going to do something else, but I can do that later; somehow you never do because there are more calls on your time and later never comes.

Sometimes it seems that I am always on the go. Sometimes it seems even my time with my Lord has to be rationed; anyway, I am too tired to concentrate when I do get there. In any case, how do I say *'No'* to people when they need help. We are told we are never to tire of doing good – we must always put others' needs first. But Lord, Mary sat at your feet to listen to you while Martha toiled, preparing a meal and you said Mary had chosen the better part. It is all so confusing, how can I do both?

Is this your experience also? Surely it has to be our priorities that need to be sorted. Our Lord knows our hearts, our thoughts; he sees that we are busy, but still he says, *'Come unto me and I will give you rest.'*

Amid the hurry scurry of life, just stop for a few moments and feel his presence surrounding you, see the love shining from his eyes saying, *'I love you my child'* – just whisper, *'Hold my hand Lord'* – and as you feel His hand holding yours, His warmth will flow into you, so, refreshed in those few moments with Him, His power, His strength will take over and the tasks that felt so heavy, are so light now, for Our Lord will be sharing the load with you.

Matthew 11: v 29-30 – *'Take my yoke upon you and learn from me, for I am gentle and humble in heart and you will find rest for your soul. For my yoke is easy and my burden is light.'*

The Emmaus Road

Luke 24: v 13-32

We have been here so many times before and usually the message is to remind us that wherever we walk in our Christian life, our Lord is always at our side. But something that has come to me recently is a little different and I think has something else to say to us.

You notice that when Jesus came upon the pair walking along the road, he first asked what their problem was. He had noticed that they were downcast, then as they relate their concern he listens, he doesn't interrupt but lets them tell the whole story, then, when they have finished, he does his very best to explain their problem, to help them to understand, referring back to the things they had been told earlier and continues on with them.

I just wonder if we are so patient with people who have problems. Do we think to ask them if we can help? Do we stop and listen, let them talk or do we get exasperated, thinking, really they should be able to understand the situation themselves, are we happy to talk them through their situation and try to help them to understand. To spend a while with them, talking further if there is a need.

In a world that seems to want to travel at great speed, many people can't seem to keep up, they become lost amidst the modern technology, yes even those – *'..if you want so and so press 1 or if you want something else press 2!'* I don't know about you but I just don't like them; it might just be that in this modern day, all sorts of problems can confuse and confound. Words and actions that were once not acceptable seem to be accepted today. So often people just need someone to stop and listen, and perhaps explain, then they can go on their way again. It may take but a few moments, but in those moments we may take away a heavy burden. Even when we are busy ourselves, let us be more ready and prepared to stop, to listen, to be helpful.

I have a piece of paper on which is written, *'One random act of kindness at a time can change the world.'* One moment of listening can lift the burden for someone who has a problem they just don't understand.

John 17: v 21

The goal is for all of them to become one heart and mind. 'Just as you, Father are in me and I am in you. So they may be one heart and mind with us, then the world might believe that you sent me!'

Where are we the church going? What impact do we have on our sad and hurting world? What witness do we give to the world? We have prayed that we as Christians will be united as one body in Christ; that we will work together to proclaim the love of God for all people. How are we doing?

Over 2,000 years ago our Lord prayed for us, that we would be one with each other and one with him as he was with his Father. He sought through prayer and did through love, his Father's will, without question. We read many times that he went away to pray; he knew the scriptures well so must have read them often. He knew his Father's will for him, and through love, loyalty and faith, casting aside all concern for himself, sought to fulfil the will of his Father. Not counting the cost; suffering pain, agony, persecution, humiliation and death. Never once was there derision between them, never once was he not at one with his Father's will, this is what he prayed for us.

It is a sobering thought for us today, that in many ways, the church is more split than ever; I don't think there has ever been so many different cults, various creeds, beliefs and doctrines, all trying to prove they are right, a variety of views and opinions, numerous and varied translations of the Bible, some good, some perhaps not to our liking, a clash of ways and ideas on how to bring people into the church, back to God.

Complacency and compromise, fighting against idealism, fundamentalism and a hundred and one other 'isms'! Ideas of closing small churches and centralizing, battling against keeping small churches open, it is difficult just trying to keep up with all the different views.

Jesus prayed that we might be one with each other as he is one with his Father; in other words, that we would love one another and work together.

The strength of the church is not in its numbers, the strength of the church is in its oneness with God and each other. The weakness of the church is not in its lack of people but the division and derision between each other within our churches and with other churches. The witness of the church obviously depends on our oneness with each other, how we work together.

God promises that where two or three are gathered together in his name, there he will be in the midst of them. This is true whether that means two or three people or two or three churches. So wherever his people meet in love, he joins them bringing power and strength to their oneness. In every meeting of Christian people, whether few or a large gathering, He is there.

No battle on a battlefield was ever won when the ranks were split, for the enemy breaks through and overcomes them. They have to stand firm, rank and file as one man for victory. If we are to present the love of God to the world and win souls to his glory, so we must stand as one man. If we don't then satan himself, it's certain, will creep in, take over and ruin the witness we try to present. Nobody can build a stable house with cracked bricks and faulty tools. Neither can we build the church of God on earth, with cracked bricks and tools that are not true. We should be the church of God on this earth. Our foundation is sure for God is our foundation and he is perfect. Our corner stone is true and perfect, for Jesus is our corner stone himself. The builder is a skilled craftsman, for the builder is the Holy Spirit, he wields the tools of love, patience, understanding, peace, joy, faith, goodness and kindness; but the builder, however skilled, cannot build with faulty materials, lacking tools and workers.

We have our foundation, our corner stone, our master builder, but what of the bricks, the mortar and tools, with which he has to build? If love, patience, understanding etc is in short supply, our oneness with each other is split, our oneness with God divided, the bricks are only seconds, the tools are not true. How is he to build?

As he strives to build the church of God to present to this sad and hurting world of ours, we do need to ask ourselves the question, *'How good are the bricks?' How strong the mortar? How sharp the tools?'* In other words, are we praying together in love, in oneness with each other, for each other? In oneness with our Lord and our God, not just occasionally but often; is our Bible fellowship at full strength? Are we studying God's Word together, in love and oneness? For we have an aim, we have a goal, to become one heart, one mind, just as our God and our Lord are one, to be one with them, so that the world might know the love of God for all people. Is that our aim in life, to bring others to a knowledge of that love?

We cannot do this as lone Christians; we need each other so desperately. We need to pray desperately together. We cannot achieve anything without prayer, we need to get this thing together, here and now; not next month, not next year, or we will move no further forward. We need to love one another with true Christian love, a love that really cares and understands, seeking to work together to build the church of God. We need to study his Word together, research it, understand it, to share our own experience of God with each other; to talk of his love together, to get to know him better together. In fact, really and truly become one with each other, one with our Lord, one with our God, as Jesus himself prayed that it would be. So let us add our prayers to his, for each other, for ourselves, that these things really begin to happen soon. Our fellowship will be sweeter, our peace will be greater, our witness louder and stronger.

So, the foundation is laid, the corner stone is in place, the master builder is waiting for the bricks, the mortar and the tools to start his work.

Jesus said, *'A new commandment I give you, that ye love one another as I have loved you. By this all men shall know that you are my disciples.'* It can only begin when we start to be good bricks, good mortar and good tools to be used through the Spirit in oneness with each other in oneness with our Lord and our God.

'My prayer,' Jesus said, *'is that they become one heart and mind, as I and my Father are one.'*

Give Us This Day Our Daily Bread

How often we hear of where we are on our Christian Journey, as if there was a road from the moment we come to know our Lord until we are called home to be with our Father in Heaven, as if each day, week, or year, marked off how far we are along our journey accordingly to how long we have been travelling.

We all walk the same path through our Christian life, how long we have been on that path makes no difference, it is literally one day at a time for each one of us. Each day is a new day with new experiences for all of us. We meet each day in God's love and guidance, that is why it is so important to be fed every day in whatever way we need, to meet the needs of that day whatever they may be.

The Spiritual bread we ate yesterday, or last week, or last year, is no good for today, any more than the material bread we ate last week will give our bodies nourishment this week. We need new spiritual bread every day, whether through God's word, prayer or fellowship.

So, friends, reach out and gather from the hand of God each crumb he offers in whatever way, that we may be spiritually fed, nourished, strengthened and ready to travel on along the Christian pathway with him.

John 12: v 32
'And I, if I be lifted up from the earth will draw all men unto me.'

That is some prophesy, but within it I see a promise, if Jesus triumphs, so too will we, for we will share in his triumph.

It was a great day for Jesus, when the Greeks asked, *'We would see Jesus'*, they were not drawn by curiosity, they had no doubt, heard about him, his healing, his miracles, his preaching and they wanted to know more; to see this man for themselves. Philip and Andrew were thrilled to take them to their friend, to introduce him to them. Are we so willing to show our Lord to others, to introduce him to others?

Our Lord looking at this little group of men saw not just a group of men but looked into the future and saw in them a mighty army of leaders, carrying the good news, seekers and future carriers of the Gospels. He even looked beyond the cross, to his own triumph. He cried, *'Now is the judgement of this world, now shall the prince of this world be cast out and I, if I be lifted up will draw all men unto me.'*

It seemed absurd to say that Jesus would win the world through a cross, triumph from defeat. Men worship success not defeat, yet Jesus, defeated in the eyes of the people, became the greatest conqueror of all time. How satan must have rejoiced at our Lord's death, no-one had even planned a decent burial place for him. His enemies laughed with delight, this man who had caused so much upheaval, so many troubles and problems to them, had gone, that was the end of him. But Jesus had said, *'And I, if I be lifted up will draw all men unto me,'* unknown to his enemies, through his death and resurrection, had been exalted and let loose in the world.

Jesus does not ask us to die in this way but he does call us to live his way, to go the way of service and self-sacrifice, then promises us that if we live our lives in his way, as he triumphed, we too will triumph. We are the seed corn of God, it is only as we die to self and are buried in our Lord's life that we can become fruitful.

When a man in criticism said to General Booth of the Salvation Army, *'Self-preservation is the first law of nature'*, Booth replied, *'Yes but the first law of grace is self-sacrifice. Whenever we spend ourselves in service to God the blessing received is far greater than the sacrifice it entails.'* Like the lad who surrendered his lunch of loaves and fishes, (not concerned that he himself would go hungry), saw a great multitude fed.

A missionary was advised that if he continued to preach it would be in peril of his life. The next morning he was met by an angry mob with stones to stone him. He asked them to first listen to his story and told of the life of Jesus from his birth to his death and his love of men. *'Now!'* he said, *'Stone me as you will,'* one by one they left, dropping their stones as they turned away.

There is power in the cross, power to draw men to Jesus. Jesus triumphed over sin and death, so shall we if we live our lives for him and as he did for others.

The last line of my favourite hymn reads, *'So shall no part of day or night, from sacredness be free, but all my life in every step be fellowship with thee.'* If we could reach something near that goal through our lives, the name of Jesus will be lifted high.

Jesus was lifted up when he ascended into heaven, but remember also the two men in white who said, *'Men of Galilee, why do you stand there looking at the sky. This same Jesus, who has been taken from you into heaven, will come back in the same way you have seen him go.'* So Jesus lifted high will return and will lift us to be with him. But the triumph is not yet complete, multitudes still pass by, heedlessly, with little concern or interest. They do not hear his pleading, *'Is it nothing to you, all ye that pass by?'* The complete triumph of Jesus rests with us, his children; it rests on our surrender to him. If by our love, our lives, our example, we lift high the name of Jesus, men and women will, like the Greeks say, *'We would see Jesus,'* then in finding him and his peace in our lives, be drawn to him themselves.

Jesus said, **'And I, if I be lifted up from the earth will draw all men unto me,'** let us strive, by our lives and witness, to lift high the name of our Lord, that his name may be glorified by all men.

Amen.

Follow Me
(Mark 10: v 17-22)

In our reading from Mark's Gospel the words that stand out for all to see are Jesus' words to the rich young man, words he had said to others on other occasions, which are, of course, 'Follow me,' words which he says to you and me.

At first glance, we may well think, that means we must love, we must be patient, understanding, caring, and all the other attributes of our Lord's life here on earth; and, of course, that is very true but I think it means very much more than that, we need to look very much deeper into what Jesus is saying to you and me.

Let's look firstly at why our Lord came to dwell among us. He came to tell us about his father, our God, how much he loved us and all people. He came to tell us about God's Kingdom, how we could taste of that Kingdom here on earth, then how we could enter and live in that same Kingdom with him after our life here on earth has ended.

He came to tell us about Salvation, how he needed to die to rise again, to overcome sin and death itself. Then Jesus went on to show his love for us by suffering all the hate and abuse of man, and his horrendous death on the cross.

He came to tell us that we only needed to believe in him. That he really had paid the price of our sin, and if we accepted the sacrifice he made then we would become righteous in the sight of God and he would be our brother and we would be heirs to the Kingdom of God.

He came to show us, by his example, how once we have accepted his sacrifice, should go on to live our lives for him in the same way that he lived his life here, which, of course, is where we first came in, to live a life of love, patience, understanding, and caring, all the attributes of our Lord's life; that is only the surface. Ah! I wonder if in fact, we are only surface Christians, living what we consider to be reasonably good lives, as far as we can, going no deeper, so that we appear to be reasonably good people and just that, well it's a start but not a very big one.

There is another reason he came. A very big reason and that was to tell people that God's love, and the sacrifice he himself paid, is for all men, women and children. Now he himself was only here for a short time and what did he say to us, his brothers and sisters? *"Therefore go and make disciples of all nations, baptizing them in the name of the Father and of the Son and of the Holy Spirit and teaching them to obey everything I have commanded you and surely I am with you always, to the very ends of the earth."*

That puts a little different light on our good lives that we live. For just living good lives will not, I fear, so enthuse those, who, as yet, have not really met with our Lord. Will people really look at us and say, 'I want to be like them, they have some happiness I haven't got, I want it for myself,' or 'they go to church and they are such lovely people, I must go also.' Will our reasonably good lives, on their own, show God's love to other people and encourage them to come and meet with our God and know his love for them? I think not.

There is a verse to a song I heard quite a while ago now, *'Lord I love you, yes I love you, Lord I give myself without compromise to you. Lord I love you, yes I love you, Make my love a fire burning in my heart for you,'* that's a bit nearer the mark, but how do we get there? It really is up to us, how much of our lives are we prepared to hand over to our God? That is a big question, for the more time we give to God the less time we can spend on our own interest, and yet until we are prepared to hand our lives over to him to do as he pleases, our lives will remain uninspiring. It will mean sacrifice, self-denial, that's for certain. It will mean much more time in prayer but where better could we spend our time than talking to someone who really loves us. I find it quite amazing that we will always find time to spend with a dear friend, because we love to share their company and we enjoy being with them, how much more should we love to spend time with someone who loves us as much as God does, or our Lord who gave all that he had for our sakes. More and more I am coming to believe that if we are to work with God on this earth, then we have to put up a united front, we have to work together for his kingdom and to do the best we can, we need to learn to love one another much, much more than we do; and I mean love not just like, or tolerate. But we, ourselves, need to change, in ourselves, in our own commitment to God, in our own commitment to each other, in our own love for God, in our own love for each other. Like the verse I quoted, *'We need to give ourselves without compromise to him.'* That means just what it says, utterly entirely, difficult of course, it is, where and when did anyone say a Christian life was easy, happy yes, inward peace yes, rewarding, satisfying but easy, that's different and yet I believe the more we allow our Lord into our lives, the more we let him take over our lives, the more we rest in him, the more we lean on him, the easier it would become for we would live our lives in his love.

Jesus said, *'Follow me,'* if we read our Bibles and seek to find the way he lived, we will see that continually, he was himself in touch with his Father seeking his will, for we are told many times that he went away to pray if he needed to pray, then how much more we need to pray. He too read the scriptures, if he needed to read the scriptures, how much more we need to read the scriptures; but above all he loved, he just loved everyone. If we are honest I think we would all admit that this is the most difficult of all things to do, to like, in many cases is not so difficult, to accept in many cases isn't too hard either, but to love? There is room for everyone in this world and we have to make room for them. Jesus said, *'Follow me,'* and that means loving everyone. In our Bible we are told that if we say we love God yet do not love others, then we cannot honestly say we love God. We need to make a start, just where we are, here and now by committing ourselves to God, without compromise. We can only do that through prayer, God will know if we are sincere in our desire to give ourselves into his hands, he knows us better than we know ourselves, so we have no secrets from him, he can see right into our hearts and minds, not only the outward show as others see us. If we are sincere he will accept our sincerity and help us, when we come to love him with our whole being then we will find that loving others will come more easily.

Jesus said, *'Follow me,'* when we do just that, then we ourselves will change and through our love will reach out and enfold others and bring them to a knowledge of God's love for them.

Jesus said, **'Follow me,'** are we prepared to do just that? If we would *follow him*, the peace, the hope, the joy, that would be ours, are far greater treasures than anything the world could offer.

Even into old age, we are his disciples

One thing that has been impressed upon me as I have tried to live for my Lord is, 'There is no retirement from Christian service' and certainly 'No redundancies,' there is always more work of some sort to be done and age is no barrier. There is no credit crunch, depression or lack of all that is needed to further the work of God's Kingdom.

It is so easy to think, 'Well I have done my bit, now it is time to sit back and put my feet up'. I know, yes from experience, that bones ache, legs and feet are tired, all sorts of aches and pains seem to appear from nowhere, sleep often passes us by, the memory plays tricks, the very word or name we are looking for is always on the tip of our tongue, one would think that we are unemployable. Not so! If we are eager and still prepared to serve our Lord he will use us and sometimes in wonderful ways we never dreamed possible.

If you are still able, charity shops cry out for help, not all the jobs are strenuous, maybe you can give only a few hours, but you would be welcomed with open arms. There are many people who would love a visitor, someone to talk to, or even someone to share a cup of tea with. Much can be done from the armchair in homes, letters or phone calls of assurance, encouragement, and sympathy, just to let someone know they are not forgotten. The list is endless, add to that list many people who need our prayers. Prayer is one of the tasks that has the greatest number of vacancies. Surely if health and strength is in short supply, there is no shortage of prayer lines that lead straight to the throne of God and they are never ever all engaged.

God takes every effort we make in love to serve him, He blesses and uses those efforts for His glory, and yes indeed, He can and will show us great and marvellous results from our efforts.

Why Lord?

Lord, I feel so flat today, why? I spent my quiet time with you this morning, but it seemed almost as if you weren't there. You were there, I know, because you always are but I just couldn't find you – Why?

I read your word eagerly, as I always do, but it said nothing to me, sometimes the words are so familiar, they just roll off the tongue, without meaning, but I know they have said so much to me in the past, why not today?

I feel guilty because my mind is dull, it's blank, it feels so empty, nothing there; why? I've tried to find you; I long to hear your voice; to hear your words of comfort and reassurance; I have a busy day ahead, I need your guidance; where, oh where are you? I feel so alone. Even my friends seem distant; it's as if they sense my emptiness. I was a bit abrupt with them, I did not mean to be, but when I said sorry they said it didn't matter, but it did, I know it did. I try so hard to explain how I am feeling, I don't think they understand though, they just shrugged their shoulders and went on their way.

Lord, when you were here, walking this earth, did you ever feel flat? According to my Bible you always seemed so alive, so switched on; nothing ever seemed to phase you out. Nothing seemed to prevent you from helping people, always a kind word for everyone you met.

Lord I know this feeling is within me and it is no one else's fault. I know even if I feel flat I must show your love to others. I know that with such a wonderful Lord and Saviour with all the promises, the hope, the peace, and the knowledge, that you are here even if I can't find you, my every moment should be filled with joy.

Lord I am human; I love you and I know you love me, but there are still times when I feel flat. Why Lord?

Sun Shine

(You are the light of the world)

Mid-January, visiting a friend, I noticed the snowdrops were up and some already in bud, only a few weeks previous many people were imprisoned in their house, unable to get out because of snow and ice underfoot; this was followed by dreary and dark days. Just a few days later the sun was shining, it was cold it is true, but how much better we felt, what a difference the sunshine makes. Apart from showing up the dust if we have been neglectful in our housework, everything takes on a new look. The birds seem to sing louder, people who looked so glum, smiled; even the trees and shrubs seem to bring forth a sign of new life.

How great and wonderful is our God in his creation, how true his promise that seasons would never change, how sure we can be that spring will follow winter then on into summer and autumn, always something exciting to see as seasons change. Soon it would be lambs, calves and baby foals, ducklings, daffodils, primroses, bluebells, new promise, new hope, it will all be there and we thank God for His continued assurance and his certain hope that is always ours .

It made me think, do we keep the promises we make? Every one of them, to God, to others, to ourselves. Are we constant and loyal in everything we do? Does our presence bring light, like the sun into other people's lives? It doesn't cost anything to smile, to laugh, to be kind, to be concerned for others. Does just seeing us and knowing we are constant, not moody, but a pleasure to be with, do we bring new hope and brighten someone else's day?

Today there is so much trouble that brings despair into the lives of so many people; which causes concern for the future. Jesus said, *"You are the light of the world, let your light shine."*

Spring follows winter, through creation we enter a very lovely season, with the beauty of an array of nature that no man could ever portray on a canvas. All at no cost to us, all a gift as a blessing from God, pray that we may shine and paint into the hearts of people we meet in our everyday life, a canvas of loveliness, straight from our hearts, freely given, it will cost us nothing and will be a gift to them through God's love for us. **Amen.**

Let Us Pray

Father God, as the light shone from the eyes of Jesus,
let the light shine from my eyes.

As he reached out and touched with understanding
and concern for others,
let me reach out and touch
the lives of others.

As the love of God poured out through His life onto others
and changed their lives,
let that same love pour out through my life
and bring joy into the lives of others.

Take me Father God,
just as I am,
work in me and through me
so that others will know your love for them.   **Amen.**

John 15: v 13
Greater love hath no-one than this, that he lay down his life for his friends

Walking in the town a few days before Armistice Day, I was pleased to see three young Air Force Cadets selling poppies to collect funds for the British Legion.

Talking to them it seemed they were very knowledgeable about the wars in which our own country was involved, way before they were born.

In an age when we are forever hearing about the sad things that are happening in our country, it was so good to meet and encourage these young people who so obviously appreciated the sacrifice that had been and was still being made, for us and them.

We are a privileged people, able to some extent to live our lives with reasonable freedom, it could so easily be different if it were not for that sacrifice that was made and is still being made by so many of our people.

Our way of life could have been so different, we could have so easily been walked all over, abused and treated as the lowest of the low; we could be ruled by men of power, ruled by an iron rod.

I am old enough to remember the stories that my father, who fought in the trenches and came home with frostbite and other injuries, told of the horrendous events that took place in that war of 1914-1918, I was fortunate he survived, if he hadn't, I would not be here.

I also remember the Second World War, two of my brothers and many people I knew, served in the armed forces, many never returned.

God's word tells us, *"Greater love have no-one than this, that he lay down his life for his friends."* Our Lord himself came to dwell among his people, to tell us of our great God's love for us, also to bring that wonderful promise of a home prepared for us with him in heaven.

Even more wonderful, he came to give his life for us, whom he calls his friends, that we may indeed know salvation and be able to live a life of peace and complete freedom. Certainly there was, and is, no greater love than his.

Wouldn't it be wonderful if, (like the three young cadets who appreciated the sacrifice made for them, by so many), people would appreciate the sacrifice that our Lord made for us, and accept the gift of love and all that it implies.

We are the people who need to stop, talk and encourage, so that the truth of God's word may lead others to the wonderful love shown at Calvary.

Does Nobody Else Care

Why is it when so much needs doing in church, nobody seems to want to help. I am sure many have experienced this.

One promises to do this or that, another is sure they can help and is quite happy to lend a hand. You contact various people by phone or e-mail; gradually the jobs are all accounted for, allotted to various members, provided all those contacted reply, all should be well and you breathe a sigh of relief, good; that means I can sleep tonight without concern.

The next few days prove you oh so wrong! Some who promised are sorry but something else has turned up and they are no longer available. Some you phoned or e-mailed have not replied even though you ask for a quick response. So once again you find yourself juggling with the various jobs. Dare you ask some who are already helping to take more work on board? You won't be popular that is for sure, so you find yourself trying to multi-task even more. Frustrated, you ask yourself that big, big question, "How much more do I have to do—*"Does Nobody Else Care?"*

Yes many of us have been there, many of us are still there, but listen friends, someone does care, God always cares, he sees, he understands your frustration. Have you talked to him about it or are you carrying the load yourself? Have you asked for his help or are you trying to cope on your own? Fretting and worrying that things will not happen as they should. Ask God for his help. He may not find you more people to help, but he might, you may well end up doing even more than you think possible, but you might not have to. God will give you the energy, the strength and the knowhow to see you through it all, so stop getting upset and frustrated, talk to God, He knows and yes, *He Does Care!*

As always the glory will be His, but yours the privilege, the fulfilment and the blessing.

Let God In!

We receive so many blessings from God, far more than we can ever remember let alone count. Endless is his love, mercy, peace, joy and forgiveness, just to name a few, and he asks nothing of us except that we love him. I believe that nothing would give him greater pleasure than if we give him more time, share more of our lives with him, give him a bigger part of our time. *Let God in*!

Time! Something which those of us who are older, thought we would have lots of when we retired, only to find we seem to have less and less. Or, maybe it is because we work slower and everything takes longer, but there never seems to be enough of it at any age.

I wasn't really thinking of service but of giving more time to talk and think of our God. Realizing and acknowledging more readily his presence with us, letting him into our everyday lives, sharing our plans and everyday activities with him.

As I talk to people there seems to be a reluctance to open up their lives, and *let God in*. It seems it is all right to take to God the problems that beset us, our concerns for others, all the worlds tragedies etc, but when it comes to the mundane things of everyday life, that is a *'No, no!'*

I have to confess I do not understand, why, when we are living the very lives God has given us, we cannot share every aspect of that life with him. I am not going to give a list of the things we should share with God, because there is no list; he is interested in and concerned for every moment of our lives. Nothing is too big, nothing is too small, to talk to God about, whether events have disappointed us or pleased us, there is always so much to say thank you for, so much to say sorry for, so many hopes and dreams to be fulfilled.

Why oh why are we content to work or even sometimes fight our way through the day on our own, and usually ending up with second best? God is but a prayer away, sadly he will stay there if we are not ready to share our every moment with him. He will not intrude in our lives if we don't invite him in, but he is eager to share our every moment.

He will help us in our dilemmas, guide us in our decisions, rejoice with us in our joy, grieve with us in our sorrows; he will add his strength to ours in our struggles.

How different our lives would be, when each precious moment is a shared moment with our God. What a difference we would make in our little corner of the world, if we took every step knowing we shared it with him. This may be a dream but it can become a reality.

Let God in; live in his power and strength.

Why Peter?

(Mark 16: v 7)

The man in white said, *"...but go, tell his disciples and Peter."* Why Peter? It was as if he didn't want Peter to be missed out. None of the other disciples were named, just Peter.

Was it because Peter had been the most loyal follower of our Lord? I think not, for remember he had very recently denied that he had any connection with our Lord. He in fact, had failed Jesus; he had acted worse than the others. I believe it was because of this that he was singled out. The last time Jesus had seen him he had been stood by the fire in tears, as the cock had crowed for the third time and Peter had been aware he had let his Lord down.

Those had been dark days for Peter since his Lord's death, not only the losing of a very dear friend but the grief of his own failure. He would have been heartbroken, deep indeed was his sorrow, even worse, he would not be able to ask for forgiveness, for his Lord was now dead. How he must have longed to see Jesus, just once more to say sorry. I wonder also, how Peter would have felt once he knew Jesus was alive again, would Jesus acknowledge him anymore? I think Jesus realized just how Peter would be feeling, so sent this message through the man in white, *"...tell Peter"* to let him know he was forgiven and still loved by His Lord.

What a wonderful word of comfort to us also, when we have failed our Lord, he still loves us, he forgives us. In fact his love is even deeper, for this is when we need him more, when we grieve over our failure. This is when we need to know his forgiveness and love for us, so that we can rise above our failure, and go forward in that love once more.

Jesus still comes today to call us back to his side, forgiven of all our failure, to tell us, he still loves even us. What a tremendous love he has for you and me, his children.

Prayer for New Beginnings

Father God, week by week, day by day, we look around our world and see devastation in so many places, we bring you our prayers for each person, place and situation, putting them into the care of your loving hands, knowing that you know the needs of each person who is suffering in whatever way. We ask for peace and healing in our suffering world.

Today we are praying for *new beginnings*, we look to our own future, trying to catch a vision of the longings and desires of our own hearts, trying to see the way forward for us, your children.

We know that we have much to confess in our failure, much to acknowledge in not having been as committed as we should have been, much we have done that has not been according to the pathway set out before us by our Lord, things we have not done that we should have done.

We have been slack in our study of your word, distant in our prayer time. Our lack of love for you and our brothers and sisters, makes us hang our heads in shame when compared to the love you have for us.

We have not loved anyone as we should have and no longer seek to bring others to the knowledge of your love for them. We hold our arms out in despair at the present day disinterest and look to the future with little hope. What can we do? We have tried everything!

We know Father, the reason for the situation we face at this moment is, in fact, the very failures we are guilty of. As we seek to bring a new phase into our Christian living, we dedicate ourselves anew to you; not just in words but also in loving action.

Bring us back from the edge of disappointment and despair before we fall over that edge and find ourselves completely lost in hopelessness.

Send your Spirit again into our very being; give us new hearts and a longing to see ourselves as your new church, afire with our love for you and your will, that we will indeed see your Kingdom come here in our lives and the lives of our community.

We know it is only when we give ourselves to you and your service that we can change the very people that we are and make the *new beginnings* we are praying for, a reality in our time.

You are our God and we your children,
Hear the prayers we bring in Jesus' name.

Amen.

When You Hurt Someone You Love

When you love someone so dearly,
In a friendship strong and true,
When the relationship turns difficult,
Because of something said by you.

When some words that you have spoken,
Words that go against the grain,
When you're feeling very guilty,
For causing hurt and pain.

When you wonder, why so often,
It's the one you love so dear,
When you speak without thinking,
Your anger has to bear.

When with love and meek humility,
Seeking forgiveness from your friend,
When in quiet contemplation,
You turn to God again.

Father God, you take control,
Help me think, before I speak,
That the precious friendship which I share,
Its love and peace may keep.

The Peace Of The Lord

When the angels sang on the day you were born,
To shepherds and sheep in the field,
The words rang out loud and clear,
Peace to the world.

When the boat rocked on the stormy sea,
With the disciples shaking in fear,
To the waves you gave your command,
Peace be still.

When you sent your disciples, to knock upon doors,
To tell of God and his love for all men.
The first words that you bid them to say,
Peace be to this house.

When after you rose from that tomb in the rocks,
Joining your friends in that room,
The very first words that you spoke,
Peace be with you.

When you said you came to bring peace to the world
To the people of long, long ago,
Today that promise is still here for us,
Peace that is given by you.

Yes Lord, I am sure that your word, it is true,
That your peace is for all who love you,
That *I AM* included in those wonderful words,
My peace I give unto you.

Prayer For A Hurting World

Father God, we live in a hurting world where many people are suffering, we listen to the radio, we watch the television, we read our newspapers. Many people are hungry and without shelter, many are abused in many ways, many live amid war torn countries, where guns and warfare are everyday norm.

We ask, "How can these things be?" When you made our world, you said it was good and it was good. What then went wrong?

We know the answer within our hearts, ever since that apple was picked from the tree of knowledge, the tree of good and evil, in the garden, man has turned away from you and turned to the things of the world. Love and concern for others has turned to love and concern for self; greed of money, possessions and power, have taken first place in life. Even we, who profess to be your children, at times wander away from you and seek the things of the world.

Father forgive us for the part we have played in spoiling your world, for our failure, for our greed, for our lack of appreciation for every blessing that we have received from your hands.

Forgive us when we don't love as we should, when we turn away from the needs of others.

Forgive us when what we give is less than the widow's mite. When we keep the bigger share for ourselves.

Remind us that Our Lord said, *"For as much as you have done it unto the least of these my children, you have done it unto me."*

But he also said *"For as much as you have **not** done it unto the least of these my children you have **not** done it unto me."*

Remind us also that we are told, "To those to whom much has been given, much will be required."

Help us to surrender to you, our life, our love, our treasure store to be used by you, as when and where you will, that many whose lives have been torn apart, may be made whole and that this world will become a better place.

Amen.

Stormy Waters

(Luke 8: v 22–25)

As they set out across the lake, accompanied by their Lord,
The water, just a ripple, the breeze so calm and still,
When, from somewhere, without warning, a mighty storm arose
Blowing the water high, very soon the boat would fill.

Their Lord he was asleep, so peaceful, unconcerned,
It seemed he did not hear the storm, as the boat rocked up and down.
Although they struggled hard to keep the boat afloat,
The disciples were so frightened, fearing they would drown.

How could he sleep so peacefully, amid the raging storm?
At once the disciples woke him and perceiving their alarm,
He speaks and bids the storm *'be still'*; he tells the wind to cease,
Obedience is immediate; the lake once more is calm.

'Where is your faith?' he asks of them *'Why be so afraid?'*
'I am standing right beside you, to keep you from all harm.'
When the storms of life assail us, when everything goes wrong,
It sometimes seems He`s fast asleep, unaware of our alarm.

But through those times of trial, that beset us through the day,
Know our Lord is with us, he will protect us from all harm.
He bids the storms to cease; to them he says, *'be still,'*
With our Lord in the boat beside us, there's no need for alarm.

In Whatsoever State

Sometimes I am so busy,
There is no time to stop,
The *must do*'s pile up so high,
They keep me on the hop.

I must do this, I must do that,
They are an endless stream,
To stop and rest a little while,
In truth, is just a dream.

So I hasten through the day,
The *must do*'s must be done,
From start of early morning,
Until the setting of the sun.

But if I were truly honest,
Then I would have to say,
That being busy all the time,
Is the way I like my day.

One Morning I rose quite early,
The day was bright and fair,
Turning the pages of my diary,
I discovered nothing there.

Some tasks had been deleted,
Some others were already done,
It was obvious from the start,
The *"must do's"* had up and gone.

For a while I felt so deflated,
To be busy, my only intent,
Then words of Paul came to me,
The secret of being content.

Whatever God's mercy allots me,
Whatever his blessings this day,
I will accept with grateful thanksgiving,
Joyful to walk in his way.

No matter how this day finds me,
Whether busy or nothing to do,
God's love still reaches out,
So he will carry me through.

In The Vineyard Of Our Lord

(Matthew 20: v 1 – 16)

On first reading of this parable, we could not be blamed if we, like the earlier workers employed in the vineyard, thought it most unfair. After all they had worked much longer hours than the last to be employed.

If it happened in any other employment I am sure there would be a strike, *"Unfair!"* would be the cry, as it is here in this parable. Words of Our Lord's that come to mind as a starting point, to put us in the right frame of thinking, are, *"Your ways are not my ways."* Our Lord's workings are very different to the ways of the world.

Time or length of time is something that is not measurable as a comparison, whether we have been Christians for many years or just a few, it does not give us any different status or reward in the work of God's Kingdom, each one of us receives the same salvation and exactly the same promises as the next Christian.

This does not mean that if we have been in the employment of our Lord for many years, we can start to take it easy, feeling we have served our time. There is no retirement or redundancy in his employ.

How *unfair*!!! But wait, how long have we been serving our Lord? Endless years? Then surely we have received endless years of peace, joy, the knowledge of God's presence and all the wonders of Christian lives, for all that length of time, whereas those who have not been in his service for as many years, have had less time to experience these wonderful pleasures.

It is not the service we give, or the length of time we serve, that is important, it is the depth of our commitment; the giving of ourselves, whether for many years or few.

What a tremendous privilege that is ours' as we experience God's love and all the wonderful blessings his love brings, there is no larger wage we could receive than this.

Life with No End

John 11: v 25
'I am the resurrection and the life'

We all know the story of Lazarus, how he was sick and the sisters had sent for Jesus to come, but he had tarried and by the time he arrived to be with them Lazarus had died, we also know Jesus raised him from the dead; this was to help them to believe.

Martha believed in the resurrection at the last day; but that seemed far away, what she wanted was to be comforted **now**, it was to this need, like every other mourner, Our Lord spoke these wonderful words: *"I am the resurrection and the life, He that believes in me, though he were dead, yet shall he live, and whosoever lives and believes in me, shall never die."*

His answer shows that he himself is the bridge of life that unites us on this earth with Heaven and eternity.

The resurrection is not far away, for it is all in our Lords hands. When those of us who believe in him die to this world we are but asleep in him and not dead. What we call dying is only crossing over the bridge into the presence of Jesus himself. Christ when he died upon the cross, abolished death once and for all. He suffered in our place, passed through the valley of darkness, leaving for us, his followers, a path of brightness.

If we could all get into our hearts the truth of the immortal life as revealed in the Gospels, it would take away the gloom and grief of the death of our loved ones. Those who live here are in Christ, those who have gone on ahead are with him, so in him we are still united. There is but one family, some whom have gone on ahead and we will follow on, soon we will all be together once more.

This truth of the endless life is one of tremendous power, when we in the smallest of ways, realize that truth. Death is not the end of anything, except mortality, imperfection and sin. Life goes on, fuller, richer, and nobler with enlarged capacities, beyond the incident, which we call death. We, like those gone before us, will never die.

Of course we miss them, for they were a part of our daily lives, of course we grieve, we are human. We remember all we shared and to us it seems all is lost. But Jesus comes to each one of us with this assurance that he is the resurrection and the life, death is no more than the continuation of our life here on earth, but in that continuation is a better life. No more suffering, no more crying, no more pain, just a life of joy, of happiness, far better than anything we have ever experienced in this life.

Our loved ones are already sharing in that better life. Let us look with renewed hope to this promise of resurrection, be happy for our loved ones who have gone ahead of us, and look with new hope to that reunion once more with them.

Amen.

Walking Through The Valley

How deep and dark the valley,
How long and tough the road,
So hard some hope to rally,
Too heavy was the load.

So quickly filled my life with doubt,
My faith, so small a spark,
It seemed the light had gone right out,
Each day seemed Oh so dark.

Whichever way the pathway led,
Whichever way I turned,
As I sought long, the road ahead,
Nothing good could be discerned.

Had My Lord deserted me?
Had he left me on my own?
The way ahead I could not see,
Had he really let me down?

He had promised always to be there,
To lead me along the way,
No need at all, for me to fear,
Just trust him for each day.

So where, oh where, could I find him?
Why hide himself away,
Why when the light seemed so dim,
Did he have to choose today?

"My Child" he says "I am right here,
I have been all the way."
"But you built a barrier of fear,
That grew bigger every day."

"You would not let me break it down,
With the love I have for you,
You chose to walk the path alone,
You would not let me through."

But Lord, I could not find you,
Although I sought so long,
I did not know what I could do,
With everything so wrong.

"If only you had come to me,
If only you had prayed,
Told me how you needed me;
You would have known – I stayed."

"So never doubt my love for you,
But talk to me each day;
Even when the way you go
Seems overcast and grey."

"Just know that I am at your side
In everything you do."
The pathways open very wide,
The grey sky's turned to blue.

Never A Moment Out of His Care

Psalm 121

We lift our eyes to the highest heavens, for our God
    is above all and over all.
Where does my help come from? It comes from this
    same God, he made the heavens and the earth,
    and he made us his children.
We will come to no harm, for we are ever in his care,
    never a moment out of his sight,
    never sleeping he watches over us day and night,
    there is nothing that can happen to us that he does not see
    and know about.
He is our shelter from anything or anyone who
    would hurt us or harm us in any way;
    night and day we are surrounded by his love and presence.
Let us remember again, Our God will watch over us
    day and night and keep us from all harm.
As we come and go about our everyday life,
    he is there to see us safely through.
Not only today but all the days of the rest of our lives.
                                                    Amen.

www.ingramcontent.com/pod-product-compliance
Lightning Source LLC
LaVergne TN
LVHW041551070426
835507LV00011B/1032